Acknowledgements

'Animals/Souls' was published i… *Words*, ed. L. M. A. Bauman-Milner, John Gledhill & Oz Hardwick (Wordspace/Indigo Dreams Publishing, 2015). 'Taking Leave' was published in *How Am I Doing for Time?* ed. Tim Ellis and Nicola Everill (CreateSpace Independent Publishing Platform 2014). 'Carp and Waterlilies at Parcival Hall', 'Petition for funding for a new tandem design, England, circa 1902', and 'No money in science' were published in *Dreamcatcher 29* (Summer 2014), 'The Ordinariness of Parrots' in *Iota 94* (May 2014), 'Octans' in *Heavenly Bodies*, ed. Rebecca Bilkau (Beautiful Dragons, 2014), and 'A long conversation' in *Envoi 166* (November 2013). 'Saturday' was shortlisted for the Ware Poetry Competition 2013. 'Ghazal for a girl I know' appeared in *Multifaith Multilingual Poems*, ed. Krishna Kumar (Gitanjali, 2008), and 'I am writing a poem', 'The date', 'Moments', and 'My grandfather's slippers' in *Truths and Disguises*, ed. Oz Hardwick (bluechrome, 2007). 'Autumn sucklings' was recorded for the CD *Tales of the Fox*, produced by Oz Hardwick and Jo Briggs (Leeds Trinity University, 2006).

'Phrase Game' is made up entirely of phrases cut out of J.M. Barrie's *Peter Pan and Wendy*, method inspired by Tom Phillips in *A Humument* (Tetrad Press 1970).

Table of Contents

The ordinariness of parrots

A book of verse beneath the bough
A flask of wine, and thou
Beside me singing …
Rubayyat of Omar Khayyam, *Fitzgerald translation.*

I am bored with parrots.

They are so green.

They flutter and shriek like graceless debutantes
shaking the leaves.
They swoop, down invisible lianas,
into big air
and up again, into another tree
active with schoolish crowds.

More shrieks.

Any minute someone will tell them
to sit down and be quiet.
How can a person recline, reading a book of poems
with a cask of wine,
when the overhanging shade
is bursting with such busy conference,
the sharing of notes, news,
the latest in preening.
All summer, this chatter boxing.
And summer after summer.

Oh to see a blackbird
or a robin redbreast
or some exotic bird like that.

A long conversation

She came at mid-morning, coffee-time. The sun was warm.
I had been watching its brightness, the splash of burnt mango
where the beams fell on the wall, and on curving damask
leaning its cheek on the light, on tobacco wood and ivory vase,

roses like papaya flesh and lemon lilies, dark lime leaves
and coconut twigs, beside the clavichord and the mandolin
and one photograph never removed. But when she came in

my eyes went out. I saw only her memories as she filled mine.
How many Renaissance mansions have we walked together,
over the years, how many fountained Persian gardens, or
places of worship, deep-domed and built over with intricate

ornament, visitors, never the worshippers, always reading
the guidebook, never saying what had to be said.
When I first knew her I cannot remember. But then something

happened. I found her later. I knew her. But I still did not know.
We were day-trippers and sightseers for a long time. And now,
when she left, I looked out, dazed at seeing the sunset. It's now.
The sun has just sunk. The sky is flushed, still, with the memory.

The sky feels the loss as no loss. The day's heat has left it replete.
All the while she turned her full revelation on me, and I, basking,
asking for more, never noticed the sun withdraw, pass overhead

shine in through the back windows, full, hot, then fade.
And now, here I stand, looking in surprise at the glow in the sky. //

Taking leave

The old man wept. It was what she had said.
He arrived as she checked down a list,
dragged cases outside, bunched keys in a fist.
The children stood by like a flowerbed.
The front door shut like a final kiss.
He sat in the sun, holding the soft wool,
hardly worn, and felt her words to the full:
He would have wanted you to have this.
The old man wept. The widow shed
her absent thoughts, her scarf and her pen.
Her hair flowed over his heart, and then
her bare arms went right round his head.
Tickets lay fallen, and the children saw
the van drawing up outside the door. ⫽

Haiku

So large
my arms, her heart.
Was it just like this
when he first took me up?

He is old
long out cold.
My boy looks. Across chasms
a touch:
and ice breaks. ///

Saving bicycles in the dark

It was late, I was cycling home. I would
have opened the squashed wooden slats
of the gate at the back, thrust in through
brambles, pushed past stacked dead wood,
feeling the swish of the grass and dandelions
springing up between the stones of the
curving path. There would be no light
but the general haze of the indirect streetlamps,
no noise but the distant sound of revellers
or the rush of cars on the street in front.
But this time,
because of the dark, I thought of burglars,
maniacs, killers and rapists, all lurking in
the brambles in the dark, my bicycle or me
the prey, no witness but the cat, twitching
at the end of the line. Just so I once paused
thinking of sabre-toothed tigers and giant
wolves, killer pigs and bears, and sought
the circle of the fire. So I opened the front
door, safe in the street and the light, clattered
the bicycle in, dust and rust on the hall flags,
and chained the door. In the morning, the
sun splashed in through the stained glass,
like a jester laughing at a thing out of place. //

Peace

Cats, babies and lovers lie
in blissful mounds, breathing. Eider down,
cast carelessly, warms. Afternoon sun
leans sideways in past curtained shades.

Carp and water-lilies at Parcival Hall

Just below there is a rose garden with pots
of paint standing by to correct mistakes.

Or maybe a Talking Beast pops its head up
onto the top level, having travelled up

the gardens that drop and drop to where
voluptuous water swells in the dry bright

woods, while ferns and foxgloves wait. It seems
a vestige of a Golden Age. Grahame's four

children pass by like ghosts. Or now, perhaps,
We are Six. Here at the apex a dragon-fly

sweeps across stiff water-lilies sitting on
a perfectly circular pond where carp go

round and round, and on the water she
sits in a stony dress, reading the two leaves

of her hands. The stone lily-pad she sits on
is edged with green. Tea-cups chime like clocks.

And then suddenly she rises, comes and takes my tea,
stands the spoon up in the cup, drinks out of the saucer.

Then she flows back, and pours herself into
the lotus position. ///

Peacock colours

She mounted the steps, slowly, like a bird,
in a dress, of cobalt blue, and a peacock shawl.
You said you wouldn't write a poem about her.
You looked at her.
Like a peacock, you said. And you observed
the setting, a garden in a fiction, poppies, old
gold flags and lupins, long green leaves, the folds
and curves of hand-made ancient bricks. She rose
up the steps, and you watched. She stood, on a
stony balcony, and looked down. Her shawl was
the colours of the sea below a high sunlit shore.
Lincoln green and aquamarine, jade and peacock,
Prussian blue, turquoise, and a seam of the sky too.

Her soft grey hair flamed round her thin beaked head.
She descended the steps not looking regal, you noticed,
but perhaps she felt she had left something behind,
or was missing the next stage of the ceremony,
or had climbed up the steps to look for her escort,
and not found him.

You wouldn't write a poem about her, you said.
But she stays written in your mind, a blue stone
set in a golden ring. ///

Woman playing a harp by a window

She curves, precisely the same as her harp.
Two men look at her through the window.
One is her twin, the other just like her harp.
What makes us think it is she indoors
and they in the street outside? They look
sad, as if they are prisoners who wish
they too could play the harp. ⫽

Moments

You and I
walk side by side.
Our long shadows go out
like Etruscan shades
to the rim of the world.

You and I
walk each side of a street, when
glaring with light
a hot stinking beast roars between us.

It leaves a gap,
warm like the bed of a bear. ⫽

The Date

The iron, like the big sleek nose of an aeroplane,
zooms over diminutive cloth. It seems
all ready for the journey, and you
look at the clock, and blood surges
as you see how close it is to take-off.

Earlier, you ironed your hair.
Plucked eyebrows, filed nails,
sandpapered legs, folded notes
very small into a tiny purse.
All this straitening and flattening,
when you mean to billow out, fly out,
take a chance, take a jump:
you know this is what you were waiting for.

You fell in love with a cageful of lions;
now the gates have been thrown wide open
and you can get as close as you like. ///

The mother

Years ago
my son-in-law
trod on a glass
at his bride's wedding.
I looked at him, and dimmed. ⫽

Afternoon

She sheered through black and white cotton satin
and through buff tissue paper, through grey lines
bolted with heavy steel pins. The scraps lay like
gems on the carpet. She put a record, with fingertips,
onto the gramophone, gingerly lowered the needle.
Trumpets in glory cried out.

Later the black and white cloth would become
a shift dress, darted and hemmed, bra straps
controlled by hand-stitched loops of cloth.
She would sit, lipsticked and ironed, by her tray
of scotch pancakes and tea, trespassing pins still
in her bosom, silent but quick.

But that other afternoon, while I watched, thinking
myself into their world, a branched line of ants,
climbing the wall, slowly the turntable hummed.
We found it much later, touch hot, and the trumpets
had melted and arched, curved like a poppadom.
They would never be vocal again. ///

Arrival in the City

Double-decker trips
past windows of many shapes,
  a glimpse, a lost glimpse
in each, a stop at a strange
street I will sleep in tonight.

My map is opened
to go to the corner shop.
  My door is bolted
against knocks I never hear,
silence, and noise from outside.

A dog without a collar,
numberless pigeons converge,
  costumes multiply,
wayward wind streaming through spring
leaves puffs out the avenues.

Scattered petals, fruit
papers, breath curling, metal
  sharded faces whirl,
chipped voices stick together,
build a monument of jazz. ///

Polis

I saw edifices
where people walked
alone
and in the lists of love.
There was no
dream more harsh
or sore than this one.
What
did they all mean
by going there,
back and forth,
in the Mall,
under the lights
of the city,
working off
the cheap chill
of the office
all day
over the hill? ///

High up in a window

For Shane

> *I saw a lady in a white smock in one of the windows on Döbrentei Square. She had cut the Communist crest out of our national flag and was waving this flag with the hole in its center. In that instant we all knew that that flag had to and would become the symbol of our revolution. For just a short moment we forgot that this was a silent march, and we cheered that lady waving the flag in the window.*
>
> *- A Testament of Revolution by Béla Lipták (1956).*

Someone cuts a hole in a flag. And leans, and waves it.

It was an impulse, a sudden chance, an instant route
into the minds of many. And having done it, having
cut it out, to hear the crowd is a drink of bright sky,
is being lifted weightless in a huge blue sky, the fog
gone of daily time, all of them a mass close as a coral reef.

And it was not that it was 1956 and she was old in Hungary
and the hole was the Hammer and Sickle, flown. It was
that all her life she had never known this would be she,
through thirty thousand days, stitch by painful stitch,
not known, one foot in front of the other, stone by stone,
past small evil alienations of day to day, used hands, toil. //

Taxis of the Marne

It makes a good watercolour, the convoy,
upright Renaults AGs. Handsome cabs, these,
smart as a Matchbox Rolls Royce, like wraiths, silver ghosts
and phantoms and later dawns. The soldiers' uniforms
match, blue-grey and red. The crowd
turns out for them in Paris, boys walk alongside –
a day out, a slow-paced fever, an exaltation.

Where does that walk go? Long miles to the river.
Fighting a saving day. While Hannibal's elephants
parade on Parisian screens. And Rome, Rome
is sacked, and Mount Etna explodes.
Mary Pickford is a coat of arms.

A boy, two boys walk beside the taxis. And there's Bambi,
and Nineteen. Eighty-Four. Little waves storming. A dead
beetle. A worm. One head, half sliced, and sideways is not a
plate of food. The sea is fallen across the flesh. They fell and
mingle not with the laughing. Head head head head head.
Leg leg leg arm arm. Why not try to hide the style behind the
dream? Is not a maggot, or a swarm of bacteria. Is a
Composition VII. Is a composition a leftover? A brain. Oh
Gertrude, Gertrude, Dad. Numbers lie numberless, cut up in
the mulchy blood and bones. Half a five upside down to an
eight. A nine, a nine, a six, seven over zero. The going down,
the going down of the, of the, of the sun sun sun.

It was a nude descent descent descent
a nude nude nude nude nude
Fallen across across the Flesh sea sea
flesh spirit spirit, drums Fallen glory tears.
remember, remember, dismember,
members dismember as years condemn
dissent dissent denuded numbers numbers buzz buzz //

Welcome

I thought we would be asking them in
into our house
a stuffy house

but they asked us outside
into their street party
I never did
anything like that before //

The stork on the hill

there is a house
on a Northern hill
not the same one
I saw before

on a Northern hill
a stork flew by
I saw before
it made me dream

a stork flew by
not the same one
it made me dream
there is a house ///

There are no more dolphins

He said, comforting me,
'There are many more fish in the sea.'
Yes
but
there are no more dolphins. ///

Ghazal for a girl I know

For Molly

Words are like sand; words allow misunderstanding,
like a wind fanned, blowing away understanding.

She has no words, but her hands are loud speakers,
loud as a band; there is no misunderstanding.

Eyes, all ears, swoop after her hands, hearing
her gestures so grand, shouting with understanding.

Eyes kiss, as her hands say which she loves
and make a stand and defy misunderstanding.

Her hands ask to be fed, her hands throw away,
they fly and land, quick as our understanding.

Her hands ask why, rejoice, hide, and show,
a laugh in her hand, truthful, no misunderstanding. ///

Seafood platter

That was the night of the seafood platter,
the night the toddler fell on his head
on a clean marble floor, the night
of throwing it all up again
and again, of the pain of
the Twin Towers on TV, the
disasters, the pain, sick, so sick.
That was the night of the dream,
the giant mussel waiting,
snarling with teeth like steam-rollers
plunging up, while the tons
of the ocean suck back
heavily on either side. ///

Animals/souls

after the painting 'Animals/Composites', by Rabindranath Tagore

He floats, sad-eyed,
on a red sea. His long beak
is like a pelican's but he
looks, too, like a rocking horse.
Above his head a cock's comb
or a horse's mane stands up
and he wears a pig's tail
or the tail of a masterful dog.
Then again, maybe this body
is merely a mirage, made up
of fractured light, or
the drawn puddles of petrol
sent out in a patch of rain.

This is just part of a listening lake,
sucking and plopping, in green and
black, a sea of sewage, gelid waste,
in each gaseous segment a soul
bobbing, the heart turned upside
down, form just a choice of echoes
now that the body's gone.

Life ripples they are, moving and vacant,
till a hand takes a brush and a palette,
wet and vivid, pungent, slapped on,
that clicks like a shutter and stops:
fossilised cave walls shut out of life. //

Death, desire, life

Did everything always dearly most beloved
end, end eventually, dreaming of true love,
and in a strain, a tune, a sinew taut so and a
thrum in the fleet night, a striven retreat, lit,
heaving up the ghost, heaven-hot of breath?

Deep in the centre, made of a magnetic clod,
enclosed in dark rock, letters let none delete,
scripts of sighings set shapes awry in sparks.
Illicit hard anvil, on which ocean-wide nuclei
rupture and reform, driven red-hot and afar,
entrap us in flames when ashes fall over fire,

let us have just this, a life-saving hot morsel.
In all life's old intricacies always here is an I
fearful of a failing, in life or the future, aloof.
Every breath of desire ends, for death or fire. ///

Octans

Eight syllables form a circle
in sand, make a planet revolve.
Pythagorean harmonies,
the do re mi of the heavens.
Strike the glass spheres, and hear them chime.
In time. And in eternity.

Divide a circle into eight.
Sailors in dark ocean ranges,
lost in the mountains of water,
bend together over the arm
of the octant, plunging lantern
lighting them, mapping their lost craft.
The south polar star in Octans
is too faint to find your way by.

Ice desert, unpopulated,
endless white night or endless day,
no music here but the white sheets
of singing snow, the chanting wind. ///

No money in science

Perhaps I shouldn't have worn
that long gown at the banquet
last night, the embroidered one
with all those alchemical symbols.
Too feminine for a man, perhaps.

I caught the attention of the Duchess.
I could see her eyes lingering,
wondering about my lapse of taste.
What's the point of studying
all this alchemy and magic,
when what really matters is the
sort of signal you're sending out
with the clothes you wear?

'I am drawn to alchemy,' I said.

But is that a good career move these days?
Only a year or so ago I heard Luther
lecture at Wittenberg . I don't know.
Is it to be magic or asceticism?

'I want to find out how to harness
the spirits of nature,' I offered,
'to make things happen; perhaps
if I really understood the spirits,
I could make carriages fly, and
speak to people the other side
of the globe, and cure the plague.'

Last night was really a careers fair,
all of us presenting ourselves
for royal patronage, and beside me
was this gloomy man, pale as
parchment, eyes like pebbles, lips
mouthing dry words: 'I will write
books about the arts of the courtier,
hunting, horsemanship, planting orchards...'

'Your ladyship,' I said, 'I read Latin, Greek,
Hebrew, Arabic. I can unlock vast realms
of secret knowledge.' I saw her cheek flush,
tempted. But the man who wants to get ahead
today doesn't touch mysteries, just keeps on
ploughing the same old furrow, head down,
reaping domestic oats.

Because when it came to the crunch,
the Duchess chose him. She took the safe man,
the man who will stock her shelves with manuals,
rather than the one who has the will and wit
to range the farthest reaches of the universe.

My grandfather's slippers

My grandfather had as a youth
a pair of bright slippers
and he went up and down
on the pavement, in the office
and through the train,
wearing them. And people looked
and looked away
and hid behind their papers
and peeped over the top.

Those slippers were
bright and hard and
a little bit scandalous. It's not
right, he ought to keep them

under his hat, they said.

But when he sat
his knees in a warped grey blanket
spilling ash
my grandfather
was glad he had them. ⫽

The Night Two Scholars Came to Visit

I was like
someone's wife, lighting
the fire – 'coffee and biscuits?' –
discreetly
busying myself in making
a comfortable ambience for your colloquy
parenthesising
with an occasional intelligent pleasantry
smiling, fetching books off shelves
lining the nest
for two such eggs as these.
I didn't even feel intrusive
I was welcomed so
by those who had something to say. ///

Prisoners

Denmark's a prison.
- Hamlet

But what about these new gold-plated ones,
they're just showing off, no need to be vulgar like that.

Then there's the prisoners who just have
a door, and a
plain window, with iron bars.
Say they want to *see things for what they are*
and *expose the lies*.
They have meetings, this lot,
worry about changing things, not happy
with the way things are, as if they could ever
change anything.
It's only natural for us to be prisoners, it's
the way things are, and always will be.
Can't go against nature.

I got a lovely stripey set last week.
We order them online.
Looked lovely on screen, and they didn't disappoint.
Candy pink and sunshine yellow.
Everyone's getting stripes nowadays.

Watched this fashion show on Prison TV,
How to look good in your cell.
Gave us lots of ideas. The warders
were like, *what are they like?*
Think we're made of money?
Ah but they love it, really.
Love to see us so excited about getting new bars
or a new padlocked door.

That's the other thing, doors.
You can get padded ones,
crushed velvet quilting, raw silk. Or this other
design, distressed blue, I like that one.

I feel it suits me.

Yesterday they were all talking about
getting doors covered in broken shell,
with an ostrich feather trim.
Lovely. Sort of reminiscent
of balls
and masks
and nights spent getting smashed.

The best kind of bar is, I think,
the one where you can create your own design.
We got this kit, the warders
set up an informal competition thing,
I nearly won it, that was a proud moment.
You can hold your head up high, in here. ///

Worms and linen

She always opens up a can of worms,
and deftly spreads the board for every guest
with stiff white linen and silver tableware.

With cookery she never came to terms.
Regarding every visit as a test,
she always opens up a can of worms.

She never sees it is her only fare
but makes it out to be a formal fest
with stiff white linen and silver tableware.

Plain to view each migrant maggot squirms
but no one has the nerve to note it lest
she open up another can of worms.

Really eating anything of course is rare,
or moving from their places even in jest
the stiff white linen and silver tableware.

This is the secret that we all must share
sitting down to face at her behest
the contents of her opened can of worms
with stiff white linen and silver tableware.

Men

I spotted three that morning
stepping out of a hole
between houses, and sniffing the air
alert, glancing about,
tossing their heads and stretching their necks
watchful of the hours
hissing and writhing ahead of them.

I moved on; but I saw them
further down, overtaking me, still gracefully necked,
shouldered and limbed, with a rhythmical lope,
and a bounce like a dynamo,
set to keep going awhile,
off to tackle the hours. ⫽

A busker admires a beautiful lady's behind

Rovers and trippers go by
in this city of tumblers and dreams,
where sweeps mourn over mountains
of fog and dew
and men with pipes
play while soldiers march
by banks
where the streets are bathed in old
yellow lamplight, and she
pauses in her Spanish shoes
and her Galway shawl.

If she loved me, would she
leave me,
tease me as she pleased me
would she flout me and delight me - ?

I cannot say.
But every night in every way
until my dying day
I will remember how she lingers
and then moves on from where I stand
singing
and watching, as she walks away,
her London derriere. ⫽

Phrase game

Wendy,
Oo!
None of us
Oo,
And you
Oo!
Wendy, Wendy,
flying about
Oo!
Wendy, there are mermaids
Mermaids!

Wendy,
just keep on saying 'I'm Wendy,'
But Wendy
had a better plan

indifferent
wildest
Wendy
'How clever I am.'

Wendy was grand.

Wendy was every inch a woman
she peeped
so
Wendy
found his button
round her neck
Wendy was shocked.

Wendy swelled with pride.
Wendy rushed to the window.
Wendy begged.
Wendy admitted.
Unfortunately
round
Wendy quite liked it

Wendy
crowing gloriously,
in solemn ecstasy.
Wendy knew
she was playing in a garden

Wendy, peeping.
Wendy
watching
became
delightfully
one;
Wendy
at the window
as small as the stars.
Wendy you may see her hair becoming white

white with
church
and Wendy
in a golden splash.

'Oh,' cried Wendy, 'to see a mermaid!'

'Wendy!' and then Wendy.
Wendy,
further
you were
Wendy. 'Ah.'

Below
Wendy
all arms
they
seized
the lust ⫽

I am writing a poem

I'm writing a poem;
but I noticed, as I came to my desk,
that the lampshades
haven't been dusted for seven years.

I'm writing a poem;
and I saw, when I ransacked the cupboard,
that there aren't any dusters
of the right type.

So I go back to the poem;
but then I ought to go and buy some dusters;
and dust the lampshades;
so I do.
There's a long queue at the check-out.

I've dusted the lampshades;
but now there are long grey tendrils
and blobs and gobbets of dust
on the carpet I hoovered this morning.
So I'll have to get the hoover out again.

Now I'm writing a poem;
but I really ought to open out the hoover,
while I think of it,
and just check that the filters aren't all clogged up.
It might be too late before I remember again.

All done. I'm writing a poem about -
but when I was looking for the dusters
I found that the cupboard was awkwardly stuffed
with all sorts of things I don't need.

Time to have a clear-out. ///

Petition for funding for a new tandem design, England, circa 1902

Gentlemen, you are of course aware
that on a tandem bicycle
in the normal position
the lady is seated behind the gentleman.

And a gentleman
feels discomfited
presenting his back to a lady.

But then
politely placing the lady in front
obliges her to steer –
an equal discourtesy.

As you see, on my model, the gentleman
would take the back seat, satisfying courtesy.
But he could steer
from the back
via a long pole, you see, thus.
No knight could be more content,
her servant and master in one.
My invention, gentlemen, is more than a bicycle.
It is the salvation of civilisation itself!

*

Gentlemen, a cigar now that business is over?
A fine sermon yesterday, I thought,
on poor misguided Eve
and on Adam's foolishness
in letting her out of his sight. ///

The jingle and the king

For Finn

'Do you think Henry VIII,' he said,
'lived his life so as to create that jingle?'

Perhaps he did. Perhaps, over the years,
he added a word now and then (well,
he was a poet, and sometimes decades
go to getting the right word) – felt, perhaps,
predestined by verse, and saw, in its
inexorable pattern, dislike, suspicion
and the mingled horror and joy
at the birth of his son. Perhaps after that
he resigned himself, knew how he was
going to have to act. Perhaps when he
married the last young woman,
in love with someone else, he wondered
and wondered about the final word.
Perhaps on his deathbed he finally got it. //

Monkey business

As Monkey went in from the garden
she was thinking about the baby bird
always not there in the garden.
The warm kitchen full
of people
coming in with bags and coats
coming in
from rooms of screens and books
coming in
from clothes and cloth and clocks.
The steam in the kitchen
the soup, the soap, the clean green leeks.
Stretches and yawns,
crashes and exclaiming.
She ran around their legs.
What am I? Guess, guess!
I'm a bird! I'm a witch! I'm a dragon!
You be a dragon
I'll be a witch.
You be a witch,
I'll be a dinosaur.
Let's go under the table.
It can be our cave.
Look, look,
I can make a funny face.
Look, look,
is this a funny face?
I can make my hair
fall over my face.
Look, look, I can do a magic trick.
Plates clattered, chairs dragged across the floor.
She thought about the baby bird. //

Saturday

Tea. Wake. Go.
(Radio), wash 7.30, cook 8.30, laundry 8.55, walk 9.10 (traffic), shop 9.18, try not to remember yesterday, (radio) kitchen 11.37, cook 11.41, lunch 12.01, walk 12.35 (traffic), library 12.50, try not to remember yesterday, find data needed 13.25, queue 13.27, walk 13.45 (babel), try not to remember yesterday, yoga 14.01, walk 15.02, post office 15.15 (announcements), queue 15.16 (announcements), walk 15.43 (babel), socialise 15.47 (clatter), leave cafe 16.21, (radio) kitchen 16.32, cook 16.35, throw out carrots 16.38, wash hair 16.41 (water), eat 17.02, (radio) laundry 17.13, fill in spreadsheets 17.47, send invitations 18.15, fill in spreadsheets 18.23, arrange party food 18.51 (babel), send texts 19.17, phone 19.26, phone 19.43, walk 19.51, phone 19.58, pub 20.13, walk 20.35 (traffic), phone 20.37, (radio) kitchen 20.59, list 21.03 (relaxation, urgent, socialising, urgent, budget, urgent, food), plants 21.17, cupboards 21.23, TV 21.45.

Reel of black and white. A waiting crowd.
Hotter and hotter, tighter and tighter,
launch, scorching hot, grey flames,
straight up into the sky,
beyond sight.

Then the moonscape, liquid rocks, soft grey hillocks
silver-edged,
dustless surfaces,
metal and light,
timelessness,
no sound.

I don't remember yesterday. ///

Autumn sucklings

i.

I've seen a fox   bound suddenly   hunch-bladed

out of the nest
    letting her fledglings hang

(at the bottoms of gardens   of leaf-moulded houses
sure as rocks surging up   from the first day   out of the loam
    foxes are seen at times)

letting her fledglings hang
    for two steps by the tongue   from the dug
        before falling   squeals pale as lavender

Is there anything you can do to   propagate the fox
            soft mouth holding the egg
planting it whole   waiting for the tree
old boxes crumpled   in a tangle of brushwood
where she lies   in her sucklings
    rain seeping out of the air   layering the bins
with earth-scent   old meat   bread-mould   wet tin tipped.
The deciduous fox   transplanted
leaves   sheds
turns out very hardy   contented with her allotment
cultivating her grub   sowing her shrimp in scabious lodgings
    just make sure she   won't soil the growing
        or root the trailing
                as with hatchlings of any kind.

ii.

So is there a fox of the week?

Well now what I have here is the
common or garden variety *vulpus vulpus*
it's a wonderful variegated red
with these bright white bits on the tip
and when you get a mass of them together flourishing
it's a spectacular sight
especially at the edge of a lawn

and the best bit is if you cut it open
there's this bright purplish flesh
streaked with pink and a delicate smell of honey

iii.

And at this time of year you get the
herbaceous mothers
pretty all in a row cockle shells on their shoes
on green-striped seats
all boarders for now in the house of the fox
and to germinate the *homo sapiens*
you need to bed them down really bed them down
with some moist compost
make sure you get plenty of nutrients in there
and you'll find they'll bud quite noisily really quite noisily

Can the panel tell me

is this really right or is there another
way to stem the running or shoot the flower?

In a case like this it just takes a semi-ripe cutting
and you get these lovely green fingers
lovely green in the limey light
then just

let them berry in the sun   let them seed.

iv.

In all humidity
  when they first rose   venal out of the sea
they found a garden   and lifted the steel
          they found a plague of locusts in the garden
they made themselves steel

but you'll find they rust down   really rust down
    and they make a very good
        sludgy muck   a good mulch
and then   just keep them pruned back
    chemical intervention is the only way really
for truly successful deracination
    try it   and if it works   then
sprinkle them with ash
    ash out the perennials   bury them in ash
                    dust them   in ash

and you'll find they don't suffer   don't suffer at all

In the late Spring   plant out your minnows
    then in these houses   witness the yield of the fox. //

Amina Alyal

Amina Alyal has been widely published in anthologies and journals, including *Envoi, Dream Catcher*, the Aesthetica *Creative Writing Annual, Heavenly Bodies* (ed Rebecca Bilkau), and *How am I doing for Time?* (ed. Tim Ellis). She has been a performer on the Northern scene for many years, at spoken word events like Spoken Word, Speakers' Corner, Spokes, Poems, Prose and Pints and Wordspace. Her collaboration with Oz Hardwick, Kaminari UK and Michael Graham has not only produced a highly successful words and music show performed to full houses in Ilkley, Wakefield and York, but also (as the group Sankakei) the CD *On an Eastern Breeze* (Catchment Recordings); and a book with Oz Hardwick, *Close as Second Skins* (Indigo Dreams). Amina's work draws its inspiration from history, from art and from daily experience, and her poems are always about new perspectives on old themes.

Other anthologies and collections available from Stairwell Books

First Tuesday in Wilton	Ed. Rose Drew and Alan Gillott
The Exhibitionists	Ed. Rose Drew and Alan Gillott
The Green Man Awakes	Ed. Rose Drew
Fosdyke and Me and Other Poems	John Gilham
frisson	Ed. Alan Gillott
Gringo on the Chickenbus	Tim Ellis
Running With Butterflies	John Walford
Late Flowering	Michael Hildred
Scenes from the Seedy Underbelly of Suburbia	Jackie Simmons
Pressed by Unseen Feet	Ed. Rose Drew and Alan Gillott
York in Poetry Artwork and Photographs	Ed. John Coopey and Sally Guthrie
Rosie and John's Magical Adventure	The Children of Ryedale District Primary Schools
Her House	Donna Marie Merritt
Taking the Long Way Home	Steve Nash
Chocolate Factory	Ed. Juliana Mensah and Rose Drew
Skydive	Andrew Brown
Still Life With Wine and Cheese	Ed. Rose Drew and Alan Gillott
Somewhere Else	Don Walls
Sometimes I Fly	Tim Goldthorpe
49	Paul Lingaard
Homeless	Ed. Ross Raisin
New Crops from Old Fields	Ed. Oz Hardwick

For further information please contact rose@stairwellbooks.com

www.stairwellbooks.co.uk

@stairwellbooks